TRIBUTE

TRIBUTE

Three Commemorative Poems

∽

Simon Armitage

POET LAUREATE

faber

First published in 2022
by Faber & Faber Ltd
Bloomsbury House
74–77 Great Russell Street
London WC1B 3DA

Typeset by Faber & Faber Ltd
Printed in the UK by TJ Books Ltd, Padstow, Cornwall

A CIP record for this book is available from the British Library

ISBN 978-0-571-38175-3

2 4 6 8 10 9 7 5 3 1

Contents

⮌

Note by the Author

⌒

The three poems collected in this edition were each written to mark significant royal occasions. There are no formal requirements of the Poet Laureate, and most of my laureate poems have been written about subjects with no connection to the monarchy. That said, there are unspoken expectations, and when I was appointed to the role in May 2019 it was suggested to me that certain momentous events were likely to take place within the forthcoming decade. Those events duly happened, and in relatively quick succession. Prince Philip died in April 2021, and I wrote the poem 'The Patriarchs' as an evocation of his generation and men of a particular character, including my own father who had died some weeks earlier. 'Queenhood' was written for Queen Elizabeth II's Platinum Jubilee in June 2022 in recognition of her seventieth year on the throne – a monumental achievement. The Queen passed away three months later, and my poem 'Floral Tribute' was composed as a double acrostic, with letters down the left-hand margin of each stanza embroidering her name into a piece about her favourite flower, lily of the valley.

Her death brought to a close the second Elizabethan era, and these three poems – one written in celebration, two as elegies – seem to represent the end of an age in terms of their subject matter, their tone and perhaps even their language. They are gathered together here and presented in that spirit.

SIMON ARMITAGE

September 2022

Tribute

QUEENHOOD

I

An old-fashioned word, coined in a bygone world.
It is a taking hold and a letting go,
girlhood left behind like a favourite toy,
irreversible step over invisible brink.
A new frock will be made, which is a country
hemmed with the white lace of its shores,
and here is a vast garden of weald and wold,
mountain and fell, lake, loch, cwm.
It is constancy and it is change:
the age of clockwork morphs into digital days,
but the song of the blackbird remains the same.

II

Queenhood: a long winding procession
from the abbey door to the abbey door.
Queenhood: vows taken among bibles and blades,
beneath braided banners and heralding horns;
the anointment of hand, breast, head, with oil
of cinnamon, orange, musk and rose; promises
sworn in secret under tented gold
so daylight won't frighten the magic away,
too sacred by far for the camera to see.
It is an undressing first then a dressing up,
a shedding of plain white cloth then the putting on
of a linen gown and the supertunica – dazzling gold foil
lined with crimson silk. Man will walk
on the moon, great elms will fail and fall.
But a knife's still a knife. A fork's still a fork.

III

———

So the emblems and signs of royalty are produced:
the gilded spurs; the blued steel sword – like a sliver
of deep space drawn from the scabbard of night –
to punish and protect; bracelets to each wrist,
sincerity and wisdom – both armour and bond.
Love is still love is still love, and war is war.

IV

And indestructible towers will atomise in a blink.
The God particle will be flushed from its hiding place.
The sound barrier will twang with passenger planes.
Civilisation will graft its collected thoughts
onto silicon wafers, laureates will trip through court . . .
But Taurus, the bull, on its heavenly tour,
will breach the same horizon at the given hour.

V

_____

Queenhood: it is the skies, it is also the soil
of the land. It is life behind glass walls
and fortified stones. Robe and stole are lifted
onto your shoulders – both shield and yoke.
Motherhood and womanhood will be taken as read.
'Multitasking' will be canonised as a new word.

VI

It is an honouring, but also an honour.
In the flare and blur of an old film
ghostly knights and chess-piece bishops deliver
the unearthly orb, with its pearled equator
and polished realms, into your open palm;
and pass you the sceptre and rod of mercy
and justice, one bearing the cross, one plumed
with a white dove; and load your fourth finger
with a ring that makes you the nation's bride;
and offer the white kid glove with its scrollwork tattoo
of thistles and shamrocks, oak leaves and acorns;
then finally furnish your head with the crown –
jewelled with history, dense with glory –
both owned and loaned at the same time.

Do those burnished relics still hold
the fingerprints of a twenty-seven-year-old?

VII

A priceless freight for a young woman to bear,
but, draped and adorned, a monarch walks forward
into the sideways weather of oncoming years.
And the heavy cargoes of church and state
lighten with each step, syrupy old gold
transmuted to platinum, alchemy redefined.
Queenhood: it is law and lore, the dream life
and the documentary, a truthful fantasy.
For generations we will not know such majesty.

THE PATRIARCHS

An Elegy

The weather in the window this morning
is snow, unseasonal weightless flakes,
a slow winter's final shiver. On such an occasion
to presume to eulogise one man is to pipe up
for a whole generation – that crew whose survival
was always the stuff of minor miracle,
who came ashore in orange-crate coracles,
fought ingenious wars, finagled triumphs at sea
with flaming decoy boats, and side-stepped torpedoes.

Husbands to duty, they unrolled their plans
across billiard tables and vehicle bonnets,
regrouped at breakfast. What their secrets were
was everyone's guess and nobody's business.
Great-grandfathers from birth, in time they became
both inner core and outer case
in a family heirloom of nesting dolls.
Like evidence of early man their boot-prints stand
in the hardened earth of rose-beds and borders.

They were sons of a zodiac out of sync
with the solar year, but turned their minds
to the day's big science and heavy questions.
To study their hands at rest was to picture maps
showing hachured valleys and indigo streams, schemes
of old campaigns and reconnaissance missions.
Last of the great avuncular magicians
they kept their best tricks for the grand finale:
Disproving Immortality and Disappearing Entirely.

The major oaks in the wood start tuning up
and skies to come will deliver their tributes.
But for now, a cold April's closing moments
parachute slowly home, so by mid-afternoon
snow is recast as seed heads and thistledown.

FLORAL TRIBUTE

Evening will come, however determined the late afternoon,
limes and oaks in their last green flush, pearled in September mist.
I have conjured a lily to light these hours, a token of thanks,
zones and auras of soft glare framing the brilliant globes.
A promise made and kept for life – that was your gift –
because of which, here is a gift in return, glovewort to some,
each shining bonnet guarded by stern lance-like leaves.
The country loaded its whole self into your slender hands,
hands that can rest, now, relieved of a century's weight.

Evening has come. Rain on the black lochs and dark Munros.
Lily of the valley, a namesake almost, a favourite flower
interlaced with your famous bouquets, the restrained
zeal and forceful grace of its lanterns, each inflorescence
a silent bell disguising a singular voice. A blurred new day
breaks uncrowned on remote peaks and public parks, and
everything turns on these luminous petals and deep roots,
this lily that thrives between spire and tree, whose brightness
holds and glows beyond the life and border of its bloom.

Note on the Author

Simon Armitage was born in West Yorkshire and is Professor of Poetry at the University of Leeds. A recipient of numerous prizes and awards, his poetry collections include *Seeing Stars* (2010), *The Unaccompanied* (2017), *Sandettie Light Vessel Automatic* (2019), *Magnetic Field* (2020) and his acclaimed translation of *Sir Gawain and the Green Knight* (2007). He writes extensively for television and radio, and is the author of two novels and the non-fiction bestsellers *All Points North* (1998), *Walking Home* (2012) and *Walking Away* (2015). His theatre works include *The Last Days of Troy*, performed at Shakespeare's Globe in 2014. *A Vertical Art* (2021) brought together his vibrant and engaging lectures from his tenure as Professor of Poetry at the University of Oxford, and, in 2018, he was awarded the Queen's Gold Medal for Poetry. Simon Armitage is Poet Laureate.

Note on the Type

This edition is printed in Centaur type, designed by Bruce Rogers (1870–1957). The type takes its name from a 1915 edition of his design, *The Centaur* by Maurice de Guérin, and draws its inspiration from Nicolas Jenson's Humanist typefaces produced in Venice, around 1470. It is regarded as among the most attractive Roman revivals of the twentieth century, and had its most notable use in Rogers' own design for the folio edition of the Oxford Lectern Bible, begun in 1929 and published in 1935.